The Himalayas

By Molly Aloian

 Crabtree Publishing Company

954.96 ALO
The Himalayas
Aloian, Molly
2
34034050000A

WITHDRAWN FROM THE LIBRARY
MELVILLE SENIOR HIGH SCHOOL

MELVILLE SENIOR HIGH SCHOOL
195669/2
LIBRARY

Apollo $16– ✓

Crabtree Publishing Company

www.crabtreebooks.com

Author: Molly Aloian
Editor: Adrianna Morganelli
Proofreader: Crystal Sikkens
Indexer: Wendy Scavuzzo
Designer: Katherine Berti
Photo researcher: Katherine Berti
Project coordinator: Kathy Middleton
**Production coordinator &
  prepress technician**: Katherine Berti

Front cover: The Annapurna Mountains in Nepal
are thought of by many as the most beautiful
mountains of the Himalayas.

Title page: Most of the Himalayan peaks remain
snow-covered year round.

Picture credits:
Katherine Berti: p. 24 (mountain)
Dreamstime: p. 16
iStockphoto: p. 27
Photolibrary: Datacraft Co Ltd: cover
Margaret Amy Salter: p. 24 (snowflakes)
Samara Parent: p. 5
Shutterstock: p. 1, 4, 7, 8, 9 (red panda), 10, 11, 12, 13 (Pangea),
  14–15, 17, 18, 19, 20, 21, 22–23, 24–25 (desert), 26, 28, 29,
  30 (all except kingfisher), 31, 32, 33 (orchid and gentian),
  34, 35, 36–37, 38 (bottom), 39, 40, 41, 42, 43, 44, 45
Wikimedia Commons: Demis.nl: p. 25; Kete Horowhenua:
  p. 38 (top); Eric Kilby: p. 9 (snow leopard); lapin.lapin:
  p. 45; Lenny222: p. 14 (map); United States Geological
  Survey: p. 13 (tectonic plates); T. Voekler: p. 33 (elderweiss);
  Vndas: p. 30 (kingfisher); Ondrej Zvacek: p. 6

Library and Archives Canada Cataloguing in Publication

Aloian, Molly
  The Himalayas / Molly Aloian.

(Mountains around the world)
Includes index.
Issued also in electronic formats.
ISBN 978-0-7787-7562-1 (bound).--ISBN 978-0-7787-7569-0 (pbk.)

    1. Himalaya Mountains--Juvenile literature. 2. Himalaya Mountains
Region--Juvenile literature. I. Title. II. Series: Mountains around the world
(St. Catharines, Ont.)

DS485.H6A46 2011   j915.496   C2011-905235-0

Library of Congress Cataloging-in-Publication Data

Aloian, Molly.
  The Himalayas / Molly Aloian.
    p. cm. -- (Mountains around the world)
  Includes index.
  ISBN 978-0-7787-7562-1 (reinforced library binding : alk. paper) -- ISBN 978-
0-7787-7569-0 (pbk. : alk. paper) -- ISBN 978-1-4271-8843-4 (electronic PDF) --
ISBN 978-1-4271-9746-7 (electronic HTML)
  1. Natural history--Himalaya Mountains--Juvenile literature. 2. Himalaya
Mountains--History--Juvenile literature. 3. Himalaya Mountains--
Environmental conditions--Juvenile literature. 4. Mountain life--Himalaya
Mountains--Juvenile literature. I. Title. II. Series.

  QH193.H5A46 2012
  508.5496--dc23
                                              2011029831

Crabtree Publishing Company

www.crabtreebooks.com   1-800-387-7650

Printed in Canada/092011/MA20110714

Copyright © **2012 CRABTREE PUBLISHING COMPANY.** All rights reserved. No part of this publication may be reproduced, stored in a retrieval system
or be transmitted in any form or by any means, electronic, mechanical, photocopying, recording, or otherwise, without the prior written permission of Crabtree
Publishing Company. In Canada: We acknowledge the financial support of the Government of Canada through the Canada Book Fund for our publishing activities.

Published in Canada
Crabtree Publishing
616 Welland Ave.
St. Catharines, Ontario
L2M 5V6

Published in the United States
Crabtree Publishing
PMB 59051
350 Fifth Avenue, 59th Floor
New York, New York 10118

Published in the United Kingdom
Crabtree Publishing
Maritime House
Basin Road North, Hove
BN41 1WR

Published in Australia
Crabtree Publishing
3 Charles Street
Coburg North
VIC 3058

CONTENTS

Words that are defined in the glossary are in **bold** type
the first time they appear in the text.

CHAPTER 1
The Himalaya Mountains

The Himalayas are a mountain range located in the southern part of Asia. They separate the Indian **subcontinent** from the Tibetan **Plateau**. They are the highest mountains in the world! The Himalayas extend for more than 1,500 miles (2,414 km) from east to west across Asia. The many exotic plants and animals in the Himalayas, as well as the mountains' astounding height have intrigued human beings for thousands of years.

Mount Everest is the tallest mountain in the world. The peak of the mountain is 29,029 feet (8,848 meters) above sea level.

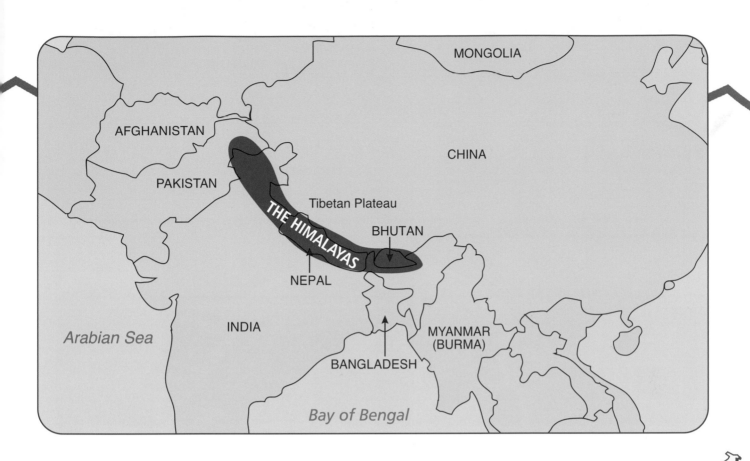

Millions of Years Old

The Himalaya Mountains are millions of years old. They began forming between 40 and 50 million years ago when part of Earth's **crust** under India slammed into the crust of Asia. The edges of the crusts were very slowly pushed upward into tall mountains. Most of Earth's largest mountain ranges, including the Rocky Mountains in North America, the Andes in South America, and the Alps in Europe, were formed this way.

FAST FACT

The word "Himalaya" means "**abode** of snow" in Sanskrit. Sanskrit is an ancient Indian language.

What is a Mountain?

A mountain is a gigantic natural landform that rises above Earth's surface. A mountain often has steep sides rising to a summit, which is the highest point or peak. Mountains are usually found in long ranges or groups of ranges called chains. They are formed in different ways, but most of the mountains on Earth have formed over millions of years. You may not be able to notice or feel it, but mountains are forming even as you read this book!

Sacred Mountains

Ancient civilizations often believed that mountains were **sacred**. For example, ancient Japanese civilizations regarded Mount Fuji as sacred and ancient African civilizations regarded Mount Kenya as sacred. The ancient Greeks believed that their gods lived at the top of Mount Olympus in northern Greece. Some of the peaks of the Himalayas are sacred in the Hindu, Buddhist, and Sikh religions.

Mount Kailash, a peak in the Gangdise Mountains in Tibet, in China, is considered to be sacred in the Bon, Buddhist, Hindu, and Jain religions. Hindus believe that the mountain is the home of the god, Lord Shiva, as well as a place of eternal bliss, and Buddhists believe that the god Demchok lives there. In Jainism, the mountain is the place where Rishabhadeva, the first Jain, was reborn and achieved freedom, and in Bon, the entire region is believed to be mystical.

NOTABLE QUOTE

"In these hills, nature's hospitality eclipses all men can ever do. The enchanting beauty of the Himalayas, their bracing climate and the soothing green that envelops leaves nothing to be desired."

—Mahatma Gandhi

Impact on Earth

Over time, the Himalayas have impacted Earth in a number of ways. They affect the **climate**, including wind, rain, and temperature, over a huge area. They also control the flow of rivers and the water supply to many areas. In fact, the Himalayas are the source of three of the world's major rivers: the Indus River, the Ganges River, and the Brahmaputra River. Half a billion people live within the **watershed**.

Millions of people in India depend on the Ganges River for their daily needs.

The Brahmaputra River, about 18,000 miles (28,968 kilometers) long, runs through Tibet, India, and Bangladesh.

Beginning in Tibet, the Indus River flows through India, Pakistan, and China.

Adapted to Mountain Life

Himalayan plants and animals are **adapted** to living in harsh mountain conditions. There are thousands of species of tough flowering plants on the Himalayas. Different types of trees grow at different **elevations**. However, no trees can grow above the tree line, or **timberline**, because the conditions are simply too cold and windy. Animals including the brown bear, the snow leopard, the panda, and the Himalayan tahr are found throughout the mountains. Their bodies have adapted to the climate. For example, the Himalayan tahr grows a dense, wooly coat in winter. Its hoofs also have a flexible, rubbery core that allows it to grip smooth rocks. A sharp rim on each of its hoofs also allows the tahr to lodge into small footholds.

In the summers, the Himalayan tahr grazes in the high pastures of the mountain slopes of the Himalayas. It comes down the mountain in the winter.

The Brahma Kamal is a species of flowering plant that grows in the Himalayas. It is named after Brahma, the Hindu god of creation.

The Blue Poppy is the national flower of Bhutan. It was discovered in 1922 during a Himalayan expedition led by British mountaineer George Leigh Mallory.

The thick fur, stocky bodies, and small rounded ears of the snow leopard are all traits that help these animals adapt to the cold mountainous environment of the Himalayas.

The red panda is a small arboreal mammal native to the Himalayas.

Part of the Himalayas

People, including Sherpas and Tibetans, have lived in the Himalayas for thousands of years. These people build homes out of rocks, wood, and earth from the mountains and consider themselves as much a part of the Himalayas as the birds and other animals. They rely on yaks for food, milk, clothing, transportation, and farming. People from other countries sometimes visit parts of the Himalayas and hire Sherpas to guide them because the Sherpas are expert mountaineers.

Mountain Exploration

Despite the harsh climate and rugged terrain, people have been exploring the Himalayas for hundreds of years. The first people to journey through the Himalayas were traders, shepherds, and pilgrims. They often crossed passes that were as high as 18,000 feet (5,486 meters) during their journeys. The pilgrims believed that the harder the journey was, the closer they came to religious **salvation**. Today, travelers and pilgrims in the Himalayas light candles, make offerings, and pray for blessings at **shrines**, monasteries, and other sacred places.

Yaks are well adapted to living at high altitudes. Sherpas and Tibetans use them to help carry heavy loads over the mountains to trade.

The Ki Monastery is a one-thousand-year-old Tibetan Buddhist monastery. It is located high in the Indian Himalayas at an altitude of 13,668 feet (4,166 meters).

Climbing Casualties

Many people have died while attempting to climb Mount Everest. Mount Everest is part of the Himalayas. It is located in Nepal. The people of Nepal call Mount Everest *Sagarmatha*, which means "goddess of the sky."

The capital city of Nepal is Kathmandu. It is approximately 100 miles (161 km) from the base of Mount Everest.

Many Mountains

There are mountains all over Earth on every single continent and in nearly every single country. Approximately 20 percent of the total land area on Earth is made up of mountains. There are even underwater mountain ranges. The Mid-Atlantic Ridge, the longest mountain range on Earth, extends through the Atlantic Ocean. The Mid-Atlantic Ridge forms a giant letter C between South America and Africa.

FAST FACT

K2, or Mount Godwin Austen, is the second highest mountain in the world, after Mount Everest. Part of the Greater Himalaya, no one has been able to climb to its summit in winter because the weather is too harsh.

11

CHAPTER 2

How Did the Himalayas Form?

The Himalayas began to take shape between 40 and 50 million years ago, but they are still considered to be a relatively young mountain range. Today, the Himalayas are still moving and changing, but they are changing much too slowly for you to notice!

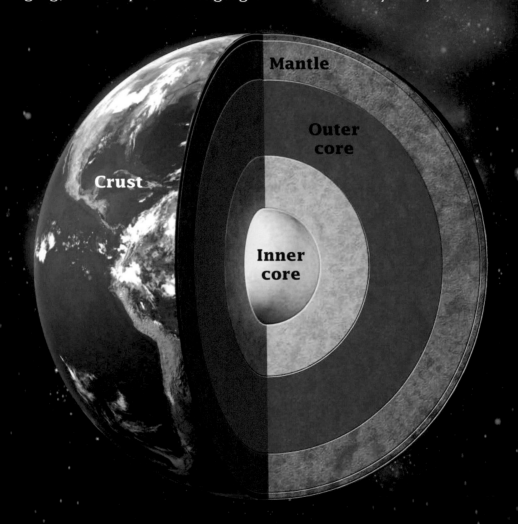

Earth's Layers

Earth is made up of different layers of rock. The outermost layer of Earth is called the crust. Below the crust is the mantle, which is a very thick, dense layer of rock. The mantle is approximately 1,800 miles (2,897 km) thick—much thicker than the crust. The outer core is the next layer. The temperature of the outer core is very hot, but the inner core is even hotter. The temperature of the inner core is about 9,000°F (4,982°C).

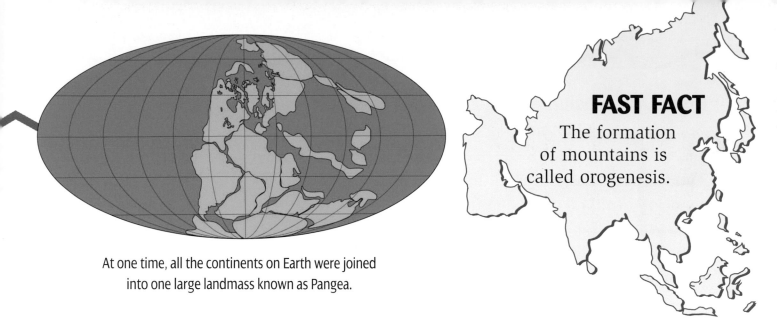

At one time, all the continents on Earth were joined into one large landmass known as Pangea.

FAST FACT
The formation of mountains is called orogenesis.

Moving Plates

Earth's crust is divided into giant slabs of rock called **tectonic plates**. These plates do not stay in the same place. They are constantly moving, which causes earthquakes and volcanic eruptions on Earth. They move very slowly, but the changes on Earth can be enormous. As they slowly move, the plates sometimes push up against one another. This causes their edges to slowly force up into gigantic folds and wrinkles—what we know as mountains. The Himalayas were formed this way. However, in order to completely understand the process we must go back in time hundreds of millions of years.

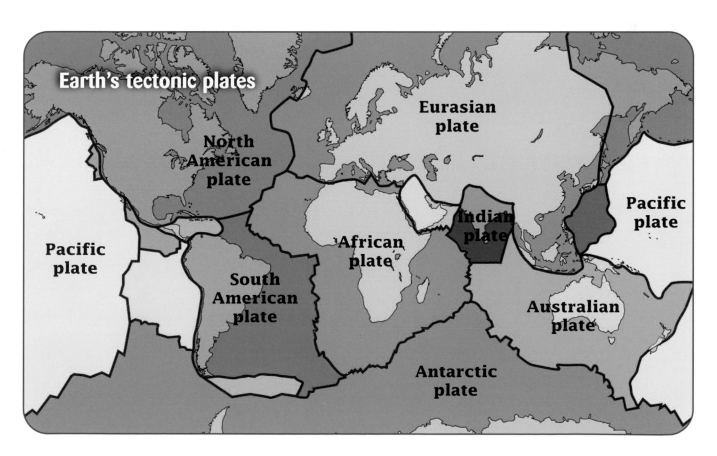

Earth's tectonic plates

North American plate

Eurasian plate

Indian plate

Pacific plate

Pacific plate

African plate

South American plate

Australian plate

Antarctic plate

Head-On Collision

Approximately 225 million years ago, India was a large island located off the coast of Australia. A vast ocean, called the Tethys Sea, separated India from the continent of Asia. When Pangea broke apart around 200 million years ago, India began to move north toward Asia. Moving just a few centimeters per year, India drifted right across the Tethys Sea from the southern hemisphere to the northern hemisphere. It smashed head-on into Tibet. The sheer force of the crash caused massive uplifting and twisting. It caused the entire Tibetan Plateau to raise 16,000 feet (4,877 meters) above sea level.

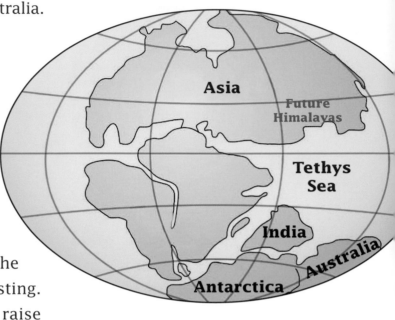

The Tibetan Plateau is the highest and largest plateau in the world, with an area of less than one million square miles (2.5 million square kilometers).

Coming Up!

Both India and Asia's tectonic plates have about the same rock density, so one plate could not be pushed under the other. The pressure of the colliding plates could only be relieved by thrusting upward. The folding, bending, and twisting at the collision zone formed the jagged, immense peaks of the Himalayas. Today, this long range of towering peaks is still being thrust upward as India continues to crunch into Tibet.

From Sea to Mountain

The Himalayas grew in a series of folds as the tough granites, basalts, and gneisses that made up the Indian plate lodged into Asia's softer, sedimentary rock. However, when **archaeologists** found the **fossils** of tiny ancient sea creatures embedded near peaks of the Himalayas, they were, understandably, confused. Plate tectonics helped answer their questions. As India approached Asia, its leading edge, made up of oceanic crust, rolled up ahead of the landmass. This oceanic crust was the first part to be lifted up, carrying the fossilized remains of the ancient ocean inhabitants with it.

The Yellow Band

The Yellow Band is a crumbly 500-foot (152-meter) layer of sedimentary rock that cuts through Mount Everest. There are billions of fossilized ocean creatures from the now-vanished Tethys Sea in the shale and limestone of the Yellow Band. It is a distinctive feature of a part of Mount Everest called the Lhotse Face.

NOTABLE QUOTE

"In a thousand ages of the gods I could not tell thee of the glories of the Himalaya; just as the dew is dried by the morning sun, so are the sins of humankind by the sight of the Himalaya."

—Skanda Purana, Hindu religious text

Raging Rivers

Some experts believe that the rivers throughout the Himalayas actually existed before the mountains took shape. They believe that the mountains welled up around the rivers. The water from these rivers followed their original courses and cut deep **gorges** through the soft, sedimentary rock. The rivers also transported countless millions of tons of silt in the fast-moving meltwater that cut its way through the Himalayas.

FAST FACT

Some geologists estimate that India continues to move north about two inches (five cm) per year. Geologists are scientists who study the structure of Earth and how it formed.

Worn Down

As soon as any mountain forms, rainwater and freezing temperatures slowly wear the mountain down. This is called erosion. Rivers carve deep valleys into rocks. Wind blows soil and small bits of rocks away.

When water freezes inside a crack in a mountain rock, it swells and can split the rock apart and break it into smaller pieces. Rockslides, avalanches, and earthquakes also change and wear down mountains.

What Is an Earthquake?

An earthquake is the sudden release of energy in Earth's crust. They are caused by the sudden breaking apart and movement of Earth's tectonic plates. The edges of the tectonic plates are marked by **faults** or fractures. Most earthquakes occur along the fault lines when the plates slide past each other or collide against each other. Some earthquakes are too small to feel, but others can cause buildings and other structures to collapse, landslides, avalanches, tsunamis, and volcanic eruptions.

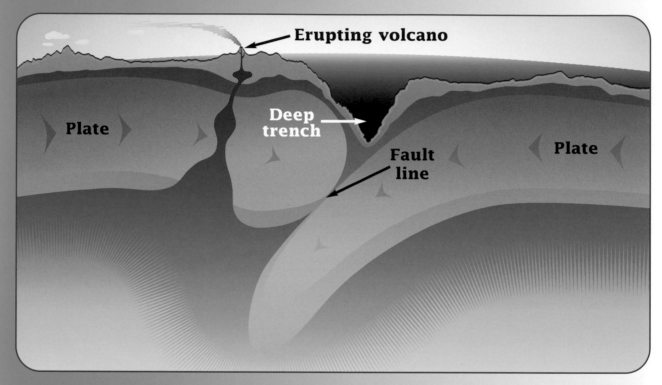

Erupting volcano

Plate

Deep trench

Fault line

Plate

Fault line

Moving Mountains

Earthquakes are common in the Himalayas. In fact, there are earthquakes nearly every day, but most are too small to feel. Approximately 900 years ago, a powerful earthquake shook the entire Himalaya region. About 600 years ago, a similar giant earthquake shook the Himalayas north of Delhi, in India. There are Tibetan, **Urdu**, and Arabic texts that tell of this earthquake and how it damaged monasteries in Tibet and Nepal, and cities as far south as Arga in India.

Releasing Pressure

Why are there so many earthquakes in the Himalayas? The Tibetan Plateau is three miles (4.8 km) high and 620 miles (998 km) wide. As the Indian tectonic plate continues to advance toward Asia, enormous amounts of stress and **friction** accumulate. This buildup of pressure keeps the crust underneath the large Tibetan Plateau unusually hot. It makes the rocks expand, which is what pushes the plateau to its very high elevation. The buildup of energy is released in the form of earthquakes.

FAST FACT

In 1934, an earthquake in eastern Nepal destroyed most of Kathmandu. It destroyed many of the homes and temples of the valley. In October 2005, an earthquake in Pakistan killed over 75,000 people and collapsed thousands of homes and other buildings.

These Tibetans survey the damage done by an earthquake.

CHAPTER 3

Weather in the Himalayas

The Himalayas act like an enormous natural weather barrier and have a huge impact on the climate of the Indian subcontinent and the Tibetan Plateau. There is heavy rain and snow on the southern side of the Himalayas, but the northern side is relatively **arid**. The weather in the Himalayas also varies greatly depending on the elevation. In general, temperatures get colder and drier as the elevation increases and warmer and wetter as the elevation decreases.

Machapuchare is a mountain in Nepal that is considered to be sacred by Hindus and is forbidden to climbers.

Summer and Winter Temperatures

The temperatures in the Himalayas vary according to region and elevation. For example, the average summer temperature in the southern foothills is about 86°F (30°C) and the average winter temperature is around 64°F (18°C). In the middle Himalayan valleys, the average summer temperature is around 77°F (25°C) while the winters are very cold. In the higher regions of the middle Himalayas, the summer temperatures are between 59°F and 64°F (15°C and 18°C) while the winter temperatures are below freezing. The temperatures in regions above 16,000 feet (4,877 meters) are below freezing. These areas are permanently covered with snow.

FAST FACT

The weather in the Himalayas changes quickly and is therefore hard to predict. All of a sudden, there can be high winds, monsoons, floods, or snowstorms.

What Is a Monsoon?

A monsoon is a prevailing wind that reverses its direction seasonally. For example, a monsoon may blow for approximately six months from the northeast and then blow six months from the southwest. Monsoons usually travel from sea to land in summer and land to sea in winter.

The summer monsoons roar through the Himalayas from the southwest and bring heavy rains from June to September.

Mountain Monsoons

The monsoon rains that originate over the Indian Ocean are drawn toward the Himalayas. As monsoon storms rise over the mountains, their moisture is released, drenching the south side of the Himalayas with more than 15 feet (4.6 meters) of rainfall each summer.

By contrast, to the north of the Himalayan peaks, summer rainfall amounts to only about one foot (0.3 meters). The mountainsides are steeper north of the Himalayas where the climate is drier. These steep slopes can cause landslides more easily and with less rainfall.

Himalayan Glaciers

There are thousands of glaciers in the Himalayas. A glacier is an enormous sheet of ice. Several of Asia's largest rivers flow from these glaciers. The frozen ice of the glaciers stores tons of fresh water. The Siachen Glacier in the Karakoram range, which is part of the Greater Himalya, is 43 miles (70 km) long—one of the longest glaciers in the world outside of the North Pole and South Pole.

This glacial lake at Kongma La pass in Nepal is fed by meltwater from glaciers in the surrounding mountains.

Changing Climate

In many parts of the world, glaciers are melting because of global **climate change**. Certain Himalayan glaciers are somewhat protected from melting because they are surrounded by high mountains and covered with debris such as pebbles and rocks. However, many Himalayan glaciers are melting as the temperature of Earth continues to increase. Climate change causes changes to monsoon patterns and melts snow and ice, which in turn, affects the water flow to some of Asia's most important rivers.

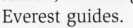

FAST FACT

On May 10, 1996, there was a sudden and terrible storm on Mount Everest. Without warning, the temperature dropped and the wind ripped across the high slopes at more than 100 miles per hour (161 km/h). The storm claimed the lives of five people who were part of a climbing expedition, including two top Everest guides.

Prevailing winds

Windward side

Leeward side

Rain shadow

Warm, moist air

Cool, dry air

Creating a Desert

The Himalayas also play an important part in the formation of Asian deserts including the Gobi Desert (right), which stretches through Mongolia and China. The desert formed because the Himalayas blocked the rain-carrying clouds from reaching this area of land. Some areas of the Gobi Desert only receive rain once every two or three years. The desert is in a rain shadow. A rain shadow is a dry area of land on the **leeward** side of a mountainous area. Rainfall and moist air prevail on the windward side of the Himalayas while arid, moisture-poor air prevails on the leeward side of the mountains.

(below) The Gobi Desert is a cold desert. Winter daytime temperatures are often below freezing.

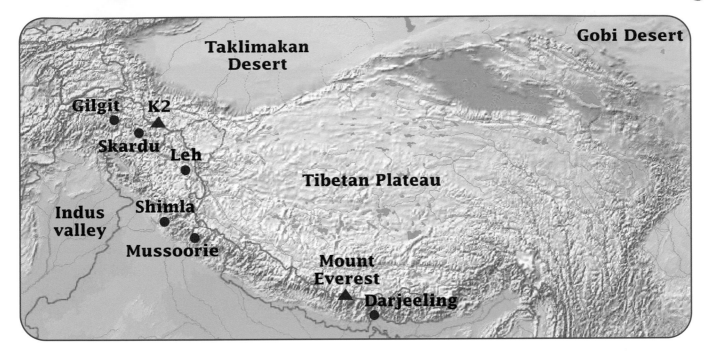

The average annual rainfall on the southern slopes of the Himalayas varies. In Shimla, in the Indian state of Himachal Pradesh, and in Mussoorie, in the state of Uttarakhand, which is in the western Himalayas, the rainfall is about 60 inches (152 cm) a year. In Darjeeling, in the state of West Bengal in the eastern Himalayas, the rainfall is about 120 inches (305 cm). North of the major peaks of the Himalayas, in places such as Skardu, Gilgit, and Leh in the Kashmir area of the Indus valley, only three to six inches (7.6–15 cm) of precipitation occurs every year.

Taking Initiative

The Climate Himalaya Initiative is a group of people and organizations interested in climate change and adaptation issues in the Himalayan mountain ranges. It was officially launched in June of 2010 in India. The Climate Himalaya Initiative does many things including advocate for a more responsible environmental governance system in the Himalaya region. They also focus on observing and facilitating climate change adaptation processes and are committed to sustainable mountain development.

CHAPTER 4
Plants and Animals

There is a wide variety of **eco-regions** in the Himalayas including **subtropical** jungles, **temperate** forests, and arctic tundra. As a result, the Himalayas are home to some of the world's most exotic species of plants and animals.

The Bengal tiger is the national animal of Bangladesh.

Himalayan Foothills

In the southern foothills of the Himalayas, there are damp swamplands and tropical habitats. There are tropical shrubs and trees such as acacia, rosewood, and bamboo, as well as tall elephant grass. The majestic Bengal tiger lives within this region. Bengal tigers are endangered because of hunting and poaching. Their habitats are also threatened because of expanding human populations. Today, there are fewer than 2,000 Bengal tigers left on Earth. At the current rate of decline, experts predict that Bengal tigers will be extinct in the wild by 2020.

The Terai

The lowest outer foothills of the Himalayas are called the Terai (also spelled Tarai). The Terai was once marshy grasslands, savannas, and forests, but **deforestation**, draining, and **cultivation** have dried out the region. People began logging the forests of sal trees in the 19th century. During this time, sal trees were an important source of hardwood timber. The hard, coarse-grained wood is durable and commonly used for constructing door and window frames.

The Terai stretches from the Yamuna River in the west to the Brahmaputra River in the east.

Temperate Zone

The temperate zone of the Himalayas rises up to about 13,000 feet (3,962 meters). Vegetation in this zone includes evergreens, oak, maple, alder, and birch. Many of the trees in this zone are covered in epiphytes such as mosses. An epiphyte is a plant that grows on another plant. The rhododendron also grows in this zone. There are 40 different species of rhododendron in the Himalayas. These spectacular plants can grow up to 65 feet (20 meters) tall.

The rhododendron is Nepal's national flower.

Indian Rhinoceros

The Indian rhinoceros is another endangered Himalayan species. Today, many rhinoceroses live in protected areas within the grasslands and floodplains of India and Nepal. At the end of the summer monsoons, the grasses in its habitat can reach more than 23 feet (seven meters) tall. Although it is protected in some areas, the Indian rhinoceros is still poached for its horn, which is highly valued in Asian markets for medicinal purposes.

Elephants in Danger

The Asian elephant is an endangered species. Poaching has impacted the population of Asian elephants. The elephants are poached for their ivory tusks, which are used to make jewelry and other items. The greatest threat to Asian elephants, however, is habitat loss due to deforestation and agriculture. Experts estimate that there are only between 28,000 and 42,000 Asian elephants living in the wild. They are listed as endangered by the International Union for the Conservation of Nature.

Elephant grass can grow to be up to ten feet (three meters) tall. It grows in dense clumps and is a favorite food of Asian elephants along with leaves, bark, and roots. The Asian elephant uses its strong trunk to pluck out a patch of elephant grass and then place the bundle in its mouth.

Coal titmouse

Sunbird

Whistling thrush

Bee-eater

Ashy drongo

Bird Land

In spring and summer, the Himalayan forests are alive with the calls of a wide variety of birds. There are more than 800 species of birds living in the Himalayas. Magpies, titmice, whistling thrushes, and redstarts make their homes in the temperate forests, while kingfishers and sunbirds can be found near waterways. Bee-eaters, drongos, and warblers are also found in the Himalayan forests.

Magpie

Crested kingfisher

Rhesus Macaque

Rhesus macaques live in the temperate forests of the Himalayas. These monkeys have sand-colored fur. Their tails are almost half the length of their bodies and help the monkeys stay balanced while moving through the trees. Rhesus macaques feed on fruits, seeds, roots, herbs, and insects in the forests.

Common Langur

The common langur is another animal of the Himalayan temperate forest. These monkeys also have long tails. Their limbs, hands, and feet are long and slender as well. Their bodies are between 16 and 31 inches (41–79 cm) long, but their tails add another 20 to 39 inches (50–100 cm) in length.

Rhesus macaques grow to be between 20 and 25 inches (51–64 cm) long and can weigh up to 19 pounds (8.6 kg).

Common langurs are arboreal, which means they live in trees. They feed on leaves, fruit, and other plants in the mountain forests.

FAST FACT

Both rhesus macaques and common langurs are considered to be sacred in the Hindu religion. They come down from the trees to roam through the temples and villages in India and Nepal, often sneaking food from people.

Beast of Burden

Wild asses, yaks, and bharals, or Himalyan blue sheep, live on the Tibetan Plateau at elevations of 14,000 feet (4,267 meters). In the past, people used yaks as **beasts of burden** while traveling on the Himalayan trade routes. People of the Himalayas still use yaks today. Yaks are extremely strong and can carry as much as 175 pounds (79 kg) to elevations as high as 21,000 feet (6,400 meters). The lung capacity of a yak is about three times as large as the lung capacity of regular cattle. The yak also has more and smaller red blood cells, which improves the blood's ability to move **oxygen** throughout the body at high elevations. These adaptations help yaks survive high in the mountains.

FAST FACT

A full grown male yak can weigh up to 1,200 pounds (544 kg).

The yak is the largest animal that is native to Tibet.

Tough Stuff

There is an abundance of flowers in the high meadows of the alpine zone. Himalayan edelweiss, orchids, and pale blue gentians sometimes cover the ground like a colorful carpet.

These plants have to be tough! In winter, they will disappear under more than 16 feet (4.9 meters) of snow. During the monsoon season, they are pelted with sheets of torrential rain. They also run the risk of being eaten by grazing animals.

Edelweiss

Himalayan orchid

Gentian

Cracking Up

Many types of insects, spiders, and mites also live above the tree line. These are some of the only animals that can live above 20,000 feet (6,096 meters). Some scientists believe that these animals live off tiny particles of food that blow up from lower elevations. They eat the microscopic pieces of organic debris and even dead insects that get lodged in the cracks of rocks.

CHAPTER 5

Alpine History, People, and Cultures

People have been living in the Himalaya Mountains for thousands of years. Many of the people living in the mountains today still live in traditional ways. People from all over the world visit the Himalayas to attempt to climb Mount Everest and the other tallest peaks.

These Tibetan women are wearing traditional clothing, including long sheepskin coats, called chubas, made of thick wool. Chubas are ankle-length, and are bound around the waist by a long sash. Many nomadic peoples of the area wear chubas, as they provide warmth in the cold mountains of Tibet.

The Newar god Kala Bhairava is depicted at the Kathmandu Durbar Square in Nepal.

Early Peoples

The Kirat were one of the earliest cultural groups living in the Kathmandu Valley. They came to Nepal in approximately 700 B.C. and ruled over the country. They were trained in the art of warfare and developed a number of towns. The Newar are also one of the earliest groups in Nepal. In ancient times, they were mainly traders. Over time, the Kirat and Newar and other ancient peoples mixed with people living in different areas of the Himalayas.

FAST FACT
The Newar population in Nepal is more than 1.2 million people.

Ethnic Groups

Other Himalayan peoples such as the Rais, Limbus, Tamangs, Magars, Sunwars, Jirels, Gurungs, Thakalis, and Chepangs live in the middle hills. They each have distinct social and cultural practices. There are many other Himalayan peoples as well. The Gaddi are hill people. They keep large flocks of sheep and herds of goats in the high hills.

In winter, they take their animals down from the higher elevations where survival is easier. They return to the highest pastures in June. Another group, called the Gujari, are traditionally a migrating pastoral people. They live off of the milk and meat from their herds of sheep, goats, and a few cattle. They find pasture at various elevations.

The Sherpas

Today, hundreds of thousands of people live in the Himalayas, but the Sherpas are perhaps the best-known mountain peoples. Their ancestors **migrated** from eastern Tibet in the 16th century. They settled in the mountains and valleys of northeastern Nepal. They based their livelihoods on cultivation and trade. They traded salt from Tibet and rice that they carried up from areas of Nepal at lower elevations. In the second part of the 19th century, Sherpas began to migrate to Darjeeling to work with British road builders and surveyors. These British **colonists** were also trying to create maps of the Himalayas, especially Mount Everest.

Namche Bazar

Namche Bazar is a village in the northeastern part of Nepal. It is located in the Khumbu Valley at approximately 11,286 feet (3,440 meters). In the narrow alleys there are souvenir shops, teahouses, and lodges for people who are on trekking expeditions to Mount Everest. There is also a weekly market in the center of the village, and people from the area come to sell their wares to both locals and tourists. Namche Bazar is one of the most famous and popular stops on the way to Mount Everest.

Tenzing Norgay

On May 29th, 1953, an exceptionally talented and tough Sherpa named Tenzing Norgay shared in the glory of becoming the first person to reach the top of Mount Everest. He shared the distinction with a man named Edmund Hillary from New Zealand. *Time* magazine named Tenzing Norgay one of the 100 most influential people of the 20th century.

Tenzing Norgay

Super-Humans?

The Sherpas are world renowned for their endurance and strength at high altitudes. How have they developed these special abilities? Part of the answer lies in the fact that they are born in the mountains and are therefore adapted to breathing the thin air at altitudes as high as 12,000 feet (3,658 meters). The Sherpas have slightly higher concentrations of **hemoglobin** in their blood so their blood carries more oxygen throughout their bodies. This means that their hearts have the ability to function more efficiently with less oxygen. The **capillaries** that feed their muscles are also denser than those of people that live at lower elevations.

Many Sherpas work as guides for mountaineering expeditions in the Himalayas.

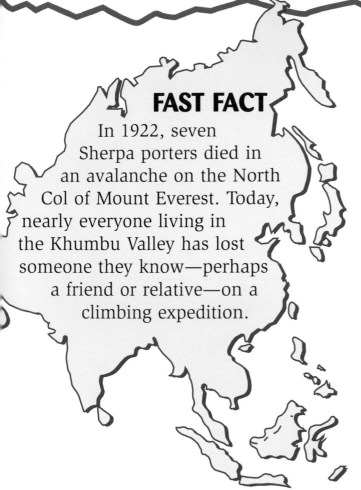

FAST FACT

In 1922, seven Sherpa porters died in an avalanche on the North Col of Mount Everest. Today, nearly everyone living in the Khumbu Valley has lost someone they know—perhaps a friend or relative—on a climbing expedition.

Chinese in Tibet

People have been living in Tibet for thousands of years. Today, about 2.3 million people live in Tibet, the highest region on Earth. Many of the people in Tibet are farmers, traders, or nomads.

In 1950, China invaded Tibet and made it into an **autonomous region** of China. The Chinese set out to undermine the language, culture, and Buddhist religion of the people of Tibet. Over the next several decades, the Dalai Lama, Tibet's most important spiritual leader, fled into **exile**, and monasteries and shrines were destroyed. Resistance by Tibetans was met with brutality. Today, many Tibetans still want independence from China.

The Jokhang Temple was constructed in the 7th century and is the holiest temple in Tibetan Buddhism. The temple was taken over by the Chinese in 1951 after the invasion of Tibet. It was temporarily used to house Chinese soldiers who destroyed many ancient Tibetan scriptures. In 1979, it's religious functions were restored, and it has been reopened to pilgrims and tourists. It is still carefully controlled by the Chinese government, however. Many police officers monitor the temple and only 100 monks are allowed to occupy the temple at one time.

CHAPTER 6

Natural Resources and Tourism

Almost one million visitors travel to the Himalayas each year for mountain trekking, wildlife viewing, and pilgrimages to major Hindu and Buddhist sacred places. Various **natural resources** are also found in the Himalaya Mountains. Natural resources and tourism contribute to the economic development of villages, towns, and cities within the Himalayas.

The Kashmir region has the greatest concentration of minerals in the Himalayas.

Kagbeni is a small village in a valley in Nepal. Crops grown in this area include buckwheat, barley, and potatoes.

Forests and Minerals

Natural resources in the Himalayas include thick forests of various trees, which are cut down and used for firewood, paper, and construction materials. Important mineral deposits include coal, mica, gypsum, and graphite, as well as ores of iron, copper, lead, and zinc.

Agriculture

Most of the population in the Himalayas is dependent on agriculture, especially **subsistence agriculture**. Agricultural land is concentrated in the Terai plain and in the valleys of the middle Himalayas. Patches of agricultural land have also been established in the mountainous, forested areas. Rice is the principal crop in eastern Terai and the wet valleys. Corn is also an important rain-fed crop on the hillsides. Other cereal crops are wheat, millet, barley, and buckwheat. Sugarcane, tea, oilseeds, and potatoes are other major crops.

FAST FACT
Food production in the Himalayas has not kept up with the population growth.

Deforestation

Deforestation to clear land for planting crops and to supply people with firewood, paper, and construction materials has slowly crept up steeper and higher slopes of the Himalayas, leading to environmental **degradation**. Deforestation is the removal of forests or an area of trees. Today, heavily forested areas are only found in Sikkim and Bhutan.

41

Almond trees (above) and walnut trees grow
on the hills surrounding the Vale of Kashmir.

Himalayan Industries

The major industries include processing food grains, making vegetable oil, refining sugar, and brewing beer. Fruit processing is also important. A wide variety of fruits are grown in each of the major zones of the Himalayas, and making fruit juices is a major industry in Nepal, Bhutan, and in the Indian Himalayas. Most of the fruit orchards of the Himalayas are in the Vale of Kashmir and in the Kullu Valley of Himachal Pradesh. People grow fruits such as apples, peaches, pears, and cherries. There is a great demand for these fruits in India. On the shores of Dal Lake in Kashmir, there are rich vineyards. People use these grapes to make wine and brandy. There are also fruit orchards in Bhutan. Oranges are exported to India.

Bananas grow in the subtropical
jungles of Nepal.

Tourists in the Himalayas

Since 1950, tourism has become a major industry in the Himalayas. The number of tourists and other visitors has increased in recent years, as organized treks to the icy summits of the Great Himalayas have become popular. Tourism is important to the local economy, but it has also had a negative impact on regions where tourist numbers exceed the capacity of recreational areas. Himalayan waterways that were once clean are now polluted with garbage and sewage.

FAST FACT

Seven Years in Tibet is an autobiographical travel book written by Heinrich Harrer. The book is based on Harrer's real-life experiences in Tibet between 1944 and 1951 during WWII and before the Communist Chinese People's Liberation Army invaded Tibet in 1950. In 1997, a movie of the same name based on the book was released starring Brad Pitt.

Countless tourists hike through the Everest region each year.

43

Protecting the Himalayas

The towering peaks of the Himalayas may be enormous and intimidating, but this entire region is extremely fragile. Climate change is melting Himalayan glaciers. Deforestation and agricultural crops are continuing to expand, and endangered animals are being poached and killed. The Himalaya Mountains need to be protected and conserved for future generations to experience and enjoy. Today, approximately 43,630 square miles (113,000 square kilometers) is under some form of protection in the Himalaya region, although only 30,116 square miles (78,000 square kilometers) are in protected areas in the International Union for the Conservation of Nature (IUCN) categories.

American Himalayan Foundation

The American Himalayan Foundation (AHF) is a non-profit organization that helps Tibetan, Sherpa, and Nepalese people living throughout the Himalayas. AHF builds schools, plants trees, trains doctors, funds hospitals, cares for children and the elderly, and rebuilds sacred places that have been damaged or destroyed. It also helps Tibetan people both in exile and living in Tibet reestablish and maintain their culture. An American investment banker named Richard C. Blum founded AHF after a trip to Tibet.

FAST FACT

In parts of China and the Middle East, there is a high demand for the body parts of Bengal tigers. Tiger skins are sold as wall hangings or rugs and tiger teeth are sold as **amulets**. The bones of tigers are used in traditional medicines.

Saving Snow Leopards

The Snow Leopard Trust is the world's leading authority on the study and protection of the endangered snow leopard. They create partnerships with communities in snow leopard habitats, assess human-wildlife conflict levels, and identify potential resources for conservation programs. The organization focuses on setting aside lands, answering critical research questions, working to change government policies, partnering with communities, and enforcing anti-poaching laws.

Bhutan Biological Conservation Complex

Bhutan Biological Conservation Complex is a network of national parks, wildlife sanctuaries, nature reserves, and biological areas covering over 5,400 square miles (14,000 square km) of Bhutan. This conservation complex allows tigers, snow leopards, rhinoceroses, and other wildlife to migrate between protected areas.

The takin is Bhutan's national animal. The Royal Government of Bhutan along with the World Wildlife Fund has created a preserve for these animals called the Motithang Takin Preserve. The protected habitat is a 8.4-acre (3.4-hectare) forested area.

NOTABLE QUOTE

The end of the ridge and the end of the world...then nothing but that clear, empty air. There was nowhere else to climb. I was standing on the top of the world."

—Stacy Allison, first American woman to reach the summit of Everest

TIMELINE

Around 200 million years ago	Pangea breaks apart and India begins to move north toward Asia.
900 years ago	A powerful earthquake shakes the entire Himalaya region.
Around 600 years ago	Another giant earthquake shakes the Himalaya region north of Delhi in India.
1590	A Spanish missionary named Antonio Monserrate draws the first known sketch map of the Himalayas.
1733	A French geographer named Jean-Baptiste Bourguignon compiles the first map of Tibet and the Himalayan mountain range based on systematic exploration.
Mid–19th century	The Survey of India organizes a systematic program to accurately measure the heights of the Himalayan peaks.
1862	More than 40 peaks at elevations exceeding 18,000 feet (5,500 meters) have been climbed for surveying purposes.
1934	An earthquake in eastern Nepal destroys most of Kathmandu.
May 29, 1953	The New Zealand mountaineer Edmund Hillary and Sherpa Tenzing Norgay are the first to reach the top of Mount Everest.
1970s	The American Himalayan Foundation is established to help Tibetan, Sherpa, and Nepalese people living throughout the Himalayas.
1975	Junko Tabei, a Japanese mountaineer, becomes the first woman to reach the top of Mount Everest.
May 1996	A sudden and terrible storm on Mount Everest claims the lives of five people who were part of a climbing expedition, including two top Everest guides.
October 2005	An earthquake in Pakistan kills over 75,000 people and collapses thousands of homes and other buildings. Surveys afterward showed that parts of the Himalayas directly above the earthquake's epicenter rose a few meters.
May 22, 2010	Apa Sherpa reaches the summit of Mount Everest for the twentieth time—a new world record.
June 2010	The Climate Himalaya Initiative is officially launched in India.

GLOSSARY

abode The place where something or someone stays or lives

adapted Changed so as to fit a new or specific use or situation

amulets Small objects worn as charms against evil

archaeologists People who study past human life through fossils

arid Very dry; not having enough rain to support agriculture

autonomous region A province-like area of a country that is distinct and has some freedom from authority

beasts of burden Animals that people use for carrying or pulling heavy loads

capillaries The smallest blood vessels in the body

climate The long-term weather conditions in an area

climate change A long-term, lasting change in the weather conditions in an area

colonists People who live in a colony, or area of land ruled by another country

crust The outer part of Earth

cultivation Preparing land for the raising and growing of crops

deforestation The action or process of clearing an area of forests

degradation Making or becoming worse

eco-region A large area of land or water containing a geographically distinct group of species, natural communities, and environmental conditions

elevations Heights that are above sea level

exile Being forced to leave one's country

faults Breaks in Earth's crust that are accompanied by a displacement of rock masses parallel to the break

fossils The remains of plants or animals of a past time that is preserved in earth or rock

friction The force that resists motion

gorge A narrow passage, ravine, or steep-walled canyon

hemoglobin A protein in red blood cells that contains iron and transports oxygen

leeward Located away from the wind

migrate To change position or location

natural resources Materials found in nature that are valuable or useful to humans

oxygen A colorless, tasteless, odorless gas, which forms about 21 percent of the atmosphere and is necessary for life on Earth

plateau A flat area of high land

sacred Describing something that is deserving of respect or honor

salvation The saving of a person from sin or evil

shrine A place that is considered sacred that people visit to show their devotion

subcontinent A large area of land that is smaller than a continent

subsistence agriculture A way of farming in which nearly all of the crops or livestock raised are used to maintain the farmer and the farmer's family, leaving little, if any, for sale or trade

subtropical Describing regions that border on the tropical zone

tectonic plates Giant pieces of Earth's crust

temperate Describing a climate that is usually mild without extremely cold or extremely hot temperatures

timberline The area of land above which no trees grow due to the harsh climate

Urdu A language spoken mainly in Pakistan and India

watershed An area that drains into a river or a lake

INDEX

FIND OUT MORE

BOOKS

Maynard, Charles. *The Himalayas (Great Mountain Ranges of the World)*. Powerkids Press, 2004.

Somervill, Barbara A. *The Magnificent Himalayas (Geography of the World)*. Childs World, 2004.

Spilsbury, Louise and Spilsbury, Richard. *Living in the Himalayas (World Cultures)*. Heinemann-Raintree, 2007.

Reynolds, Jan. *Himalaya (Vanishing Cultures)*. Lee & Low Books, 2007.

WEBSITES

Himalayan Alpine Biome
www.blueplanetbiomes.org/himalayanalpine.htm

WWF—Eastern Himalayas
www.worldwildlife.org/what/wherewework/easternhimalayas/

Global Environment—Biodiversity—Alpine Biome
www.admwebstudios.co.uk/Biodiversity7.htm

Snow Leopard Trust
www.snowleopard.org/

WITHDRAWN FROM THE LIBRARY MELVILLE SENIOR HIGH SCHOOL